BITTER PILLS

E. Martin Pedersen

1. blue fish swim under
the blue sea as we discuss
our separation

2. after the wildfire
I emerge from the well
with only my name

3. I was so happy
when I bought the new shoes
that don't really fit

4. nobody calls me
to walk in the sun, I wait
but nobody calls

5. I mistook mushrooms
for monuments – and that made
all the difference

6. cat on the slippery
soapy bathtub rim
watches the bubbles sparkle

7. deep in the grass
praying mantis
sits out the storm

8. powerlines –
water droplets
shaken off one bird
land on another

9. kitten in a trance
believes sweater to be
the holy mother

10. concrete sidewalk ...
that trail a snail leaves
shows the way home

11. the he-bird and she-bird
sit under the dragon flower
touching bellies

12. tiger mosquito
also charges
the lighted window

13. head down, head up —
deer continues grazing
yet knows when to run

14. defeat looms
when ant carries a leaf
bigger than an ant hole

15. wolf ...
as if food could ever give
what hungers it

16. cat in the corner —
eyes sparkle like a soldier
right before a kill

17. jaguar so happy
when white bunnies
circle the tree

18. the gang at work hums
alone, silent and searching
ant walks away, lost

19. driftwood on the sand
wave from the sea floor —
surf's up!

20. guitar –
caught in a web
of fingers

21. boiled cabbage
style counts

22. lovely smelling soap that does not clean

23. white carnation
crushed out like a cigarette
on asphalt

24. watermelons and onions —
a feast that keeps on feasting

25. between match head
and striking surface
there's a hesitation

26. entering a clean-smelling house
feel for a light switch

27. childless mother
on the crumbling cliff
watching tide wash in out

28. do other wives
fight their husbands
while reading The Awakening?

29. man feels cold
not wearing his coat
carrying it

30. at the politician's funeral
you had to push your way in

31. the alcoholic and the hummingbird
eye each other

32. how sorry how sorry
is the hiker
who set the forest ablaze?

33. two ugly people
look at selfies
smile

34. in Candyland
where everything's candy
the winners get vegetables

35. walking in a Kyoto park
thinking about a woman
a petal lands on my forehead

36. globes of seafoam
in glittering sunlight
distort my view

37. at the bank
surrounded by people
without headaches

38. African violets
mother cultivated …
they grew for her

39. when we married
she had beautiful teeth
hair the color of weeds

40. your breast slips
out of your blouse
as I help you off the ground

41. after you left
it snowed all week
on the cemetery

42. you see pretty flowers among weed clumps
I see weeding

43. your delicious perfume
gave me a migraine
that never ended

44. my happiest day
you pick a fight

45. to kiss the violinist's neck

46. contemplating busy ants
I miss my bus

47. we talked about our father dying
then changed the subject

48. I hug my guitar when
I should be hugging you

49. all my adult life
I have waited for the word:
malignant

50. I owe letters
to old friends and family —
nonetheless I sing

51. you know you're there
where the horizon intersects
the sunset

52. rain on the island
wrapping me twice

53. forest night —
I go in deeper

ACKNOWLEDGEMENTS

1. Paper Wasp, Summer 2012.

2. cattails, January 2014 (Editor's Choice Award).

3. Failed Haiku, November 2016.

4. Taj Mahal Review, December 2013.

5. Valley MicroPress, November/December 2013.*

6. Bear Creek Haiku, #152, 2019.

7. Under the Basho, November 2016.

8. Wales Haiku Journal, Winter 2018.

9. Bear Creek Haiku, #111, 2012.

10. Modern Haiku, January 2019.*

11. Bear Creek Haiku, #151, 2018.

12. Taj Mahal Review, December 2013.

13. First Literary Review - East, March 2019.

14. First Literary Review - East, March 2019.

15. Lyrical Passion, April 2016.

16. Failed Haiku, November 2016.

17. Taj Mahal Review, December 2013.

18. Poetalk, August 1999.*

19. Taj Mahal Review, December 2013.*

20. Lyrical Passion, February 2013 (Best of the Best Haiku Prize).

21. Failed Haiku, January 2019.

22. Bear Creek Haiku, #152, 2019.

23. Valley MicroPress, November/December 2013.

24. Ink Sweat & Tears, May 2015.

25. First Literary Review - East, March 2017.

26. Bear Creek Haiku, #111, 2012.

27. Bear Creek Haiku, #111, 2012.

28. Valley MicroPress, November/December 2013.

29. Taj Mahal Review, December 2013.

30. Ink Sweat & Tears, May 2015.

31. Beechwood Review, August 2017 (Touchstone Award nominee).*

32. Ink Sweat & Tears, May 2015.

33. Chrysanthemum, April 2017.

34. Ink Sweat & Tears, May 2015.

35. Under the Basho, November 2016.

36. Bear Creek Haiku, #151, 2018, #152, 2019.*

37. Sonic Boom Journal, December 2016.

38. Taj Mahal Review, December 2013.

39. Valley MicroPress, November/December 2013.

40. Failed Haiku, November 2016.

41. First Literary Review - East, March 2017.

42. hedgerow, November 2016.

43. Ink Sweat & Tears, May 2015.

44. Creatrix, March 2019.

45. Beechwood Review, August 2017.

46. Beechwood Review, August 2017 (Touchstone Award nominee).

47. Bear Creek Haiku, #151, 2018.

48. Bear Creek Haiku, #151, 2018.

49. Ink Sweat & Tears, May 2015.

50. Bear Creek Haiku, #151, 2018.

51. Failed Haiku, January 2019.

52. Bear Creek Haiku, #151, 2018.

53. Creatrix, March 2014.

* slightly revised